SESAME

SESAME

POEMS BY JACK MARSHALL

COFFEE HOUSE PRESS :: MINNEAPOLIS :: 1993

Earlier versions of some of these poems originally appeared in *The Amer-ican Poetry Review, Berkeley Poetry Review, The Bridge, Caliban, Exquisite Corpse, Five Fingers Review, Manoa, Pivot, Ploughshares, Poetry Flash, Sifrut, Talisman,* and *Zyzzyva.* The title poem of this book, "Sesame," appeared in *The Pushcart Prize Anthology, 1991-1992.*

The publishers would like to thank the following funders for assistance which helped make this book possible: The Bush Foundation; Dayton Hudson Foundation on behalf of Dayton's and Target Stores; The Gen-eral Mills Foundation; The National Endowment for the Arts, a federal agency; The Lannan Foundation; The Andrew W. Mellon Foundation; Star Tribune/Cowles Media Company; and The McKnight Foundation. This activity is made possible in part by a grant provided by the Minne-sota State Arts Board, through an appropriation by the Minnesota State Legislature. Major new marketing initiatives have been made possible by the Lila Wallace-Reader's Digest Literary Publishers Marketing De-velopment Program, funded through a grant to the Council of Literary Magazines and Presses.

Coffee House Press books are available to the trade through our pri-mary distributor, Consortium Book Sales & Distribution, 1045 West-gate Drive, Saint Paul, MN 55114. Our books are also available through all major library distributors and jobbers, and through most small press distributors, including Bookpeople, Inland, and Small Press Distribu-tion. For personal orders, catalogs or other information, write to:
Coffee House Press
27 North Fourth Street, Suite 400
Minneapolis, MN 55401

Library of Congress Cataloging in Publication Data

Marshall, Jack, 1936-
    Sesame : poems / by Jack Marshall.
       p.   cm.
     ISBN 1-56689-015-2
     I. Title.
   PS3563.A722S47   1993
   811'.54—dc20   93-26494, CIP

10   9   8   7   6   5   4   3   2   I

TABLE OF CONTENTS

SESAME

Again, for Naomi and David,
and in memory of my mother,
Grace Cohen Marshall

PART ONE

COILED SPRINGS

One winter's end, love gone cold in Cleveland OH, I roamed
south past the battered shoe
on the ground, flattened glove in the road, and somewhere

near to onionskin-thin lilac, reached
that honeysuckle swollen Florida sky. . . .
It stretched round an orange-

pulp concentrate doled out a drop
each dawn we hauled
and hoisted hundred-pound iron coils

onto a huge metal drum unspooling, curling,
snipping rows of pliant springs
inside a frame suspended

from a ceiling rail feeding it
slowly, shakily
by a single chain

into the furnace from which would emerge hardened
steel. One day a radiant
bed-frame sliding out overhead

missed the track
and hung there,
glowing

instant
solar fire,
then dropped, near

3

white-
hot cinder
teetering on edge, raw, quivering

rip in the seam of day-
light's casing not eight feet away. It's taken
more than twenty years to see

the shadow of that wrought wavering
flame beside me now
I see now

I don't see now invisible now
blazing
core which, if not fed on again

and again, I'd have to feed
a first and last time both
at once. In a blink, a second's

no more
than it takes
to be consumed and still

there, while here
is flesh
recalling it-

self ash,
instant ex-
tinguishment

had not quick, hook-toting mill-hands
propped and steered it away.
No wonder since then a bed

is also a door
you enter at night on your back
into the other world, eyes

following the angular, migrant,
sexless women anonymous in faded denim
squatting in cabin doorways, shrinking,

tightening like fired, coiled springs, flinty
eyes inviting
you in

or out where bales of hay beginning
to simmer and hiss
underneath

a summer shower ripening
into downpour, make it seem anything
and everything possible is near.

CANNERY
(De Kalb, Illinois)

Easy to lose
       a hand
as a finger there where the scythe-curved
scooper in the hands of a lineman—
sun-shrunken, from as far south as the Gulf—
collected an incessant rain
of cans still hot from fusing
with whirled-on caps, stacked onto carts
headed for the oven. . . .

               Day and night
a deafening shooting gallery, clattering
tin cans down through metal chutes from one
AM CAN CO. boxcar after another
pulled up along the siding. . . .

                  Hard
rain from above, steaming water up to the ankles, we'd stand
for hours on the nod, too exhausted and sleepless to feel
the hissing forklift tires
roll over our toes. Like being force-fed
a harvest from heaven while standing in hell. . . .

And there was always some damn fool
who couldn't keep from sticking his hand into that ingesting
mess of gear-shafts to keep the glutted
works from snagging, as in a magnate's backed-up gullet. . . .

                              While up in the rafters,
sending down this corn-
ucopia of peas and carrots from the Corn Belt,

                                        the lucky
quality inspectors made out, smoked, pissed
the mixed blessings of their youth into the simmering
    vats.
Grade A approved. Ship it out.

CRANE

Tonight I want to return to Elizabeth,
New Jersey, where Stephen Crane lies
under a stone, and my father,
after twenty years of skimping wages, finally
opened his own dry-goods store.
I worked there after school, on weekends,
but it didn't take a genius to see
from the sad look of the place—
dim light, threadbare "goods"—where it was headed.
In all the time I spent in that smog-sucking town
of wan bargain hunters and hangdog merchants,
I never knew of, let alone visited,
Crane's grave. Then, I was more enamored of
that other Crane, Hart (lovely name!),
whose grave is the belly of the South Atlantic.
Besides, I couldn't imagine any reason why
anyone would want to stop off, never mind
die, in Elizabeth, New Jersey. It seemed
nobody there cared about, much less
knew, the color of the sky.

VOYAGES

Now that there's no time at all for her,
there's less for you

to remember
leaving one early summer morning—

sun on the sidewalk, the broken
red bricks of Brooklyn, flowers brilliant in the yards,

clinking unbuckled infantry boots ringing
down the street, stirring dead-ends to voyages. . . .

How thrilling it felt to be definitely
going places, though not so sure

what places, with no plan for early return,
and the grey O of her staring

disbelieving face at the porch window, who'd
uproot her roses in a rage, throw out

your stained microscope slides and prized stamps,
weightless, leaping wildlife in brilliant tropics.

They follow you soon after you leave
into the garbage amid a buzzing

both insect and human,
where memory, heaped, steams, taking

root in that place we begin
by calling home.

GREEN

Heat in the park today, almost an African heat. . . .
Saw green as something we remember with,
and tonight see miners in Johannesburg just about now

blink, stepping out into broad daylight, as they pile into trucks
headed for their shanty townships under the shadow
of armored police "hippos". . . .

While all around others go
full tilt into romance, careers, breakdowns, lawsuits,
I am taking the night

off, time out . . . though so little
am I of my time
it doesn't even notice

I'm missing. Something in me
would rather let the night pass
through; would stroke and play with,

rather than pilot it, because up ahead
or nearby there's a moment
never more

green, more strongly felt
than when the past is dropped,
but now is gripped

by the fatal, fixed attention
of career killers with the fire-
power of gods at their fingertips, who can switch

night into day, day into blinding desert; men dead-
set on planning war with its two choices: victory
and the unknown.

The way children see
everything, being themselves
unseen, tonight I can be told things

you have not told anyone, since I will not
be here long enough to haunt you
with its revelation.

After weeks besieged by news,
today, over a beer, I heard
someone call the heart

"Beirut of the body." Such poetry
the future has in store! In my notebook
I find: "Don't sink to the bottom,

settling for muck. While you mull
this over, mouthing the words
without having them

swim straight into your bloodstream,
it's just an idea, and life hasn't
grabbed you by the throat yet."

THE REST OF IT

Menaced like all the mute, unborn,
unconceived mothers
yet to be, still happiness
calls to us, and summer

will come and each one
do their utmost to duplicate
themselves in flesh and other
works of the imagination,

as someone in a frenzy
of fragments finds himself
needing to be whole again.
Out of a tireless effacing

blue, flowers steadily
gathered, given, soon lose
their fragrance, the hand
withdrawn, and touch

forgotten. Out of the
mousy bustle, on the strained,
mulch-mortared wall, memory
shakes and vertigo

crumbles, summing up
the years, erasing them. . . .
What paradise there is, then,
comes with a vengeance, the last

pain feeling no worse
than the first, no
less. And waking midway between
blood and burnt orange

dawns set in emerald lakes
creates a chemistry which works
up more azure than we can
foresee or imagine

we lack. Happiness is
what we wish for, ongoing, given
enough time for uninterrupted,
sustained amazement; as though

overhead, a great circling
gull, wild, white-winged, floats
without forethought. No small
wonder then such a place

found in map or logbook
lets us watch the sky
go nowhere, only flowing
azure to emerald

green grass underfoot
in the same instant we wake
to laughter though we have
much to lose besides a foothold

near where rapid waters meet.
Halfway to the dream
we came here for, we'd rather sleep
if we could, through the rest of it.

WHAT TOOK PLACE THERE
—for Ken Richardson

Fully extended in flight, midafternoon
bird shadows, like handkerchiefs
after the departing, thrown
on sunlit windows. . . .

                Summer's not here now,
but in the whistling air's
a trace. . . .

   Is it this sudden
hint among leaves catches
glints
of those sea-sprayed days you knew
you'd need to call up again?—holding
while sending on ahead;
even then, about to become
memory, like foam in your arms, fading. . . .

   Not childhood, but as free
of ambition or mistrust there
in that summer lodge on the cliff-
edge of the continent where having come to
an end of flight, the body could begin
new life, new friendships,
and what we could no longer hold
of our pieced-apart lives
we let go, stripping the anxious
circuitry of our minds among shimmering
bare bodies wavering

down the path to the beach where naked
flesh was firm
sunlight, and mist
condensed into a rainbow, double-
arched overhead, and we within it. . . .

            To live beside ocean
air is to absorb extra-
terrestrial dimensions: pulse, perspective, elongate;
breath taking on a heartbeat boundless
as twilight glows on long
after reds and blues disappear
and swallows skim
drinks of water from the fountain pool. . . .

               We faced that shifting
weight containing all
the water eyesight can hold, permanent
present containing the past of the planet
and future, if it wasn't already
all around us, afloat, time
made visible, the god we see
never full-face. . . .

            Time is dirt
cheap, you said, that's why
it's so precious. . . .
                  And each day
equaled our gratitude for it. . . .

                  All clear in that light,
nothing was forbidden, no one left out;

neither in tree-house, nor loft, nor in deep meditation
could you be interrupted, only joined
by friends, their fine-tuned
antennae; each as near
to others as to himself, all
together eyes closed, feet up, on that terrace
level with the lazily flapping cormorants
surfers called "the Mexican air force."
Morning and sundown we watched
the sea's upturned, unlidded eye
staring back, shrugging its massive muscle-
bound shoulders with abandon,
and what it abandoned
was time. . . .

    Not to paint an earthly paradise,
but under certain conditions, what's given
exceeds the desired-for: unbidden, fragrant
meals materialize out of thin air; weddings
danced around over a heaping
dish of hash; a joint passed
hand to hand mimics Michaelangelo's
Creation, God's fleshed
lightning-rod finger poised
to touch the about-to-be-
inspirited Adam, while flutes whittled
from nearby canebrake weave
birdcall, wavecurl, and one tap
on the drum releases the new
rhythm as you feel yourself
entering a tide at work
without ever tiring. . . .

As there are times
when thoughts you've come to alone
can be spoken only in company,
so at times what you hear
yourself speak in company
you would not have come to alone.
Nor to the nights that are for feeling pleasure
more thickly; girls, beautiful
but sometimes barely
conscious, gliding in beside you as they did
through unlocked doors now
crumbling into a seafloor
deeper than memory can follow. . . .

    Those nights and days you wished
would stay, but they were going;
while out past the pleasure islands,
Oahu, Maui, doper's paradiso,
thousands of miles west in the Asian muck
replayed nightly on TV, that deadly
storm of shrapnel and napalm
no amount of wishing away could make a dent in,
was ongoing. . . .

    Wondering, then, if in the days further on
it would at last be clear
what took place there,   here
they are, more than you bargained for,
yet there's so much
gets away all the time
in trying to hold on. . . .

Comes a day when a drug-maddened naked one,
clinging to the stone flower
urn's rim at the garden's edge,
like a freaked-out infant
clutching a cement tit,
must be pried loose
from the wheel steering all—
less through vision than vertigo—
toward a sky-blue that absorbs
all tarnishing and terror. . . .

       Now a thermal kites
a wing spreading wide,
and over the treetops, slips. There
at the heart of the hum fallen
mute, what you have all along
intensely imagined is nowhere
visible in the steady throbbing. . . .

       In everyone, you recognize
a bit of yourself, and all of
yourself you recognize
in no one, or is it the many
in the one whom you don't have
the luxury of leaving behind, with never
any direction but back

into the fold, the always were, are, will be
stars, thinness of evening's
last violet veil dividing
laughter from slaughter,
and writing, this slipshod shoe-

horn into the unknown holding more lives
than history knows. . . .

        Somehow nothing
but the visions that haven't yet
materialized are good
enough now.

PART TWO

SESAME

Delectable little seeds
freckling the round cookies' crown—
kaa-iik, in Arabic, strands of skin-
smooth dough pinched together
end to end, each a circle
fitting in the palm of the hand;
speckled with anise seeds, baked
in the oven, golden brown.

·

Weeks later, I still have the shoebox
filled with them you left for me.
These last years, each new batch made
smaller, thinner,
by your hands that near the end
had to see for you
instead of your eyes that saw,
you said, "only smoke."

·

After each visit I'd bring my stash
on the plane back to San Francisco
and in my kitchen dip one,
then another into coffee, lingering
over them—hard, edible
chunks of dust; inside, a horizon
taste of anise, after-
taste of the black licorice

we were addicted to as kids. Daily
dust we used to munch on
for hours, without their giving out,
kept in the battered tin can on the stove.

.

Over dishes piled with them,
women gossiped, planned weddings;
men discussed business and argued
the minutest variations of religious law.

Now I ration and savor
each one, since they're growing scarce,
and the recipe has disappeared
along with the maker.

.

Her cooking pots and pans—dented,
discolored, burnt black—
over the years took on
character, each taking on
a different face and shape,
like friends I'd recognize
in her small apartment. Kitchen folk,
who'd served her more than fifty years.
Friends of the family, in
and out of the fire.

.

Having arrived too late,
coffin already closed,

I missed seeing you
a last time.
Later, took a keepsake
from your dresser—
the old pair of scissors,
handles' black enamel
wearing off—I now use
to cut the manuscripts
you never saw, and trim
the beard you made a face at
on first seeing.

Make another face. Any
of your many mocking ones . . .
I wouldn't mind.

        •

Laid in ground, July's end
evaporating, in slow-
motion recall: her never asking
"What's on your mind?"
but *"Ish fee elbak?"* Arabic for
"What's in your belly?"—question
whose grasp of the real
does not depend on any answer.

        •

"Phish elbak" ("Satisfy your belly")
she'd urge me to
go out into the street
when she'd find me poring over

my microscope and slides,
staining an insect wing, or after
one of my successful chemistry experiments
which stunk up the house. . . .

          But I was already
happy, like the roaches
inside the walls
with a little garbage.

        •

Excess honey
crystalized in the aluminum foil
lining the can of baklava
she'd urge on me and I'd protest, having
too much luggage for the plane-ride back . . .
and now, late as usual, remorse
a near miss,
am glad I brought it.

      Shaved slivers, thick
sugar chunks like coarse silver-streaked
quartz, sticky, fragrant with rose-water . . .
I pinch out
and melt under the hot tap
from the kitchen sink.

I have no use now
for so much sweetness.

        •

Long-distance
calls I used to make to you on Sundays . . .
I'll miss them,

and, as they say, regret
my lower phone bill.

•

She used to tease me:
"If you lost your mind
you wouldn't be losing much."

•

At the cemetery, nodding
toward the expensive pink marble
headstones among rows of grey slabs,
Louie says, "When you're alive
people are not so good to you,
but after you're dead
they're very good. In death,
they're terrific."

•

September sun, lower
earlier each day,
and a hard sowing
wind high in the trees. . . .

Now summer,
which did not come,
is not going to.

•

After eighty years, she still cannot read
or write a word in English or Arabic,
not having been to school, either
in Beirut or Brooklyn.

•

In more than fifty years, she absorbs
a few simple words in English the way sand
absorbs water, and peppers her Arabic
with mockeries of the language
in which she feels herself a reluctant
refugee.

Mimicking Pop's "Don't give me a lecture,"
with "Don't give me a rupture."

•

Another moon shot.
After the first man was landed,
she said, "Let's see them land a man
on the *sun!*"

•

After managing to scratch her name
in English (lower case, predating ee
cummings), a painstaking

scrawl, barely
legible enough to qualify
for citizenship papers back when,
she promptly put pen and paper down
ever after.

•

Her illiteracy, a kind of stubborn
immobility.
        Obstinate
power of the old
          to say *No!*

•

Sad, the way old faces change so much
we can no longer detect in them
any similarity to our own.

•

In the absence of a tape, impossible to reproduce her speech.
Spoken Arabic comes from far deeper
in the throat than English, or what she often scornfully
   referred to as
"Frenjy": all that is quaint, mannered, and ultimately
worthless.

•

Hawked, gargled, spit: Arabic,
arid and vivid at once. Desert parched
down to a mineral grit where dryness hones things to an edge.
Gutturals and consonants grind stones,
pulverize enemies into a pinch of snuff;
the stuff old Arab men stick up their noses.

        •

Odd, from that place you did not see to here,
but from this place you see to there. If so, where
go to be seen

here?

        •

In the Koran, "Paradise
is under the feet
of your mother."

Paradise may be
all lust. If so, then aren't we al-
ready in paradise. . . .

        •

At times now absently turning on the afternoon soaps
and game shows. Like you, watching without seeing,
listening without watching, leaving on without listening,
colored flicker, canned laughter.

At your grave we joked
about putting in with you your beloved
TV.

       •

You keep coming back
to her whom you came from and fed on
and left.
           She herself is gone. Now
you are not *from* any more, but *to*.

       •

Passed on. But not gone? Okay then,
withdrawn—as God
is that which we have
to do without. For the faithful, God
becomes all
the dreams one
never acted on.

All fresh grows
old. God
or word, what-
ever you cannot live or face,
you're told.

       •

Pop used to chide me: "You want things easy
and want to find things out for yourself."
Both true.
And what I have found out for myself is that
things are not easy.

•

Curses in Arabic, secret weapons,
incendiary
burrs attaching to the hated one and burning
through the genetic
channel of assholes descending in time
back to his ancestors.

•

Founded not on feast or famine,
Islam is a fire in the bowels,
extinguishment of the senses.
No wonder Rimbaud's
headlong
rush into that inferno.

•

Curses' portable
stream of fire
to annihilate
an enemy's traces
as surely as the desert
wipes out footprints.

•

We ought to study curses
to know what lies in store for us.

•

What would have become of Rimbaud in reverse—
after Africa, poetry. . . ?

•

How tired of speaking, how exhausted
from appearing you must have been.

How the older people grow, the more they carry
their entire body's
weight in their faces.

•

Ike telling about his father:
how in the hospital after a massive heart attack,
the old man (an avid cardplayer) in a coma
kept repeating, "Give me an ace, give me
a king, a queen,
give me a heart, give me a heart . . ."

an hour later, gone.

•

A certain logic of feeling?—
that what we hear leads us to want to hear more?
Forms a pattern oddly familiar

yet alluringly strange; leaps on us
in welcome
surprise or fearful dread, words that must be
made to flow as easily as water; aqua
architecture, going through
you back to the beginning
before taking a next step forward.
Words that can sometimes rescue
if you're lucky
enough to be surprised by them.

•

On TV, the young woman in Istanbul,
after terrorists had gunned down a group of worshipers in a
    synagogue,
quips, "My mother is Jewish, my father is Muslim;
we have our own Mideast
crisis at home."

•

Yehudi Arabi.
Arabic Jew.
Ox-
    ymoron.

•

In the future
slum or kingdom
come, never-

mind the doves, the
wolves will do
fine.

Only let
streets and alleys
not be just wide
enough for one,
in which no two
can meet.

·

Lately am getting practice in peering
into people's eyes at eight in the morning
at the clinic, putting in Mydriacil drops
to dilate their pupils.

In my white pants and Nikes,
patients call me "doctor."
I don't correct them.

Most people squirm in their seats, flinch at the drops
that sting. But the old Asian women from Vietnam and Laos,
slender as young girls in their wraparound, flower-print skirts,
sit quiet and still when I lean forward with the dropper;
unblinking, having seen far worse, they stare straight ahead.

Photos of the eyes' interior
show light pockets of fluid and dark craters,
nerve webs, blood vessels, like the moon's surface.
Or solar coronas, helical patterns like the rings of Saturn.

Any of them could be your
cataract eyes.

                    •

Passing the cemetery, an elderly woman
greets a mother and her two small boys.
Crooning, "My, my, how you boys are growing fast!",
she turns away, so that only I can hear her
mutter under her breath, "To what,
I don't know!"

                    •

Under blue sky, red-breasted robin standing on sprinklered
groomed grass . . .
as if the colors, day's variation of the rainbow's
seeds, could heal once.

And for all.

PART THREE

GRAVESEND

I would do anything to please
her smile, nightly
grease of my dreaming, who spoke

as though words were renewable
weddings in summer's heat-
dance, green and dirty brown

lots borderless with evening running down
to the bay beyond the outfield foul lines ex-
tending to infinity; briny, teeming

salt tang of space
opening like bells, now
drifting near, now farther out, chiming.

In the bitter cold,
when I approach, I'm often old
and don't stay. But piecemeal as recall,

I won't be swerved from
regressing with the key which fits
all locks to be sprung

open at the end. Her never again
to look out the window on a summer day, happy
dog, adoring boy, the lazy lolling

love which does away with
here, there, now, later. . . .
You can see it

in the way a mother sits, a child
stares, both
pairs of rapt, devoted eyes

folded into one
heart's core. No one else
there. From afar, the world

calls, cold puffs in a dusk that's the same
ebb everywhere. Playing late in the park,
or just walking in the street, like being naked,

or heading home through firefly sparks in the dark
you feared would suddenly turn to foam. . . . Go on,
it's the wind between skins that lets through

air, as the leaf lets go
by its stem. Try
the knob; it's in every breath. Any error may unlock

a future of terror, or erase it.
Better see
with the blue

of more than merely eye-
sight the white
mystery of fright stay behind; see

a whirling fall of leaves gather,
standing open like a gift
of new time brought

down from the sky.
Anything now not of the body, lies.
Gleaming snow, tumbling sea is what you want

out there, not souring your own
sweetness you can't help
spill

like mother's milk. I am there,
but there is not me. . . . Then,
who is it

blurs and disappears
and reappears as the boy I was?
Or does the boy glance up

from a daydream to see
for an instant himself
suddenly here?

G-D

Is how we unspelled it back then, taboo-
Loaded, defused for secular use,
While the rabbis, all beard and black cloth, hovered

Overhead, gall-breathed, stick-wielding
Watchdogs shadowing the pages we scrawled on
Omitting the one-

Forbidden o-
Void vowel, hollow
Between consonantal poles, short-

Circuiting powers of the unutterable
Name the eye does not reach and words turn back from

Together with the mind.

———

Those raised, ready sticks—broad as two-by-fours—
Pried from the backs of hardwood chairs, struck
Open palms, clenched fists, deep stinging

Whacks if you lost your place in the reading of the sacred text.
One summer day, dodging a random blow, a headstrong boy
Leaped out the classroom window to the ground

Two floors below, picked himself up with a curse
We'd utter only under our breath

And hobbled off, never to return.

———

Ancestral, perennial, penitential,
Bred-in-the-blood diet
Of denials, feeding

On exile's endless
Minus sign, subtraction
Of all feeling but the mute

Recognition: before the first step is taken,
The end is reached; before the tongue moves,

Speech is finished.

—

I can even now hardly bring myself
To spell it whole, so fiercely
Did those scowling fanatics guard against the invisible

From taking form.

—

Ha-shem, we said in Hebrew, meaning the Holy Name.
But in English the veiled vacancy more visibly
Renders the withheld power of what is not there.

Chaos—down to the microscopic
Mess of atomic elements and molecular mayhem—is ordered
Creation compared to that minuscule black

Slot housing wormhole loops and branches bridging
Worlds lost to us down micro-networks of space and time,
As many as there are

Motions, motion creating forms, forms
In motion, constantly
Deforming, reforming

Singularities just below a horizon
All depth but not yet
Given birth to a wealth of light.

—

What might you have said
Had you been allowed to
Speak? What might you have thought

Had you been allowed to think?
And, forgetting what you were supposed to
Know, what knowledge might not flow

And, like all pleasure and science that heals, fly
In the face of Tables of the Law?

—

Unapprehensible, unapproachable
Creator of the universe permanently

Out of the galactic lariat
Loop that filling in would cinch and knot: the nothing-
If-not-worlds-wanton

Original ovum
Circled by astral tadpoles
Drilling to the core. . . .

Though no Rimbaud, this I know:
O echoes,
Enlarging space, its mother-

Moaning *A* beginning to brim
Molecular messengers already
Full-grown bodies on the nuclear lattice. . . .

Hung by a thread, the same moment
Opening them to the tame household deities
Opens to the whirlwind

Gods that have no name.

THE GREEN LAMB

The sky, when all else fails,
sometimes permits this:

late afternoon sun going not only
down but doubly

brilliant, bulging
rays solid as any

blinding metal off the sea,
and in it light

you thought would not return,
gathered plump as a trumpet-call from summer's

and your own infancy, glints
off the green-glazed, ringletted lamb

your brother brings out: "Remember this?"—salvaged
from her last few effects.

As it was, so is it still:
the hollowed plaster thorax cavity

that used to hold pencil nubs, clips, household
bills by the fistfull . . .

Open-eyed all those days and nights,
it took in whole those years

you stared—holding your breath—long past it
and out the window into dimensionless home-

sickness. In air, in space, in time and bone—
a habitation: you would not call it

home. Squinting more, seeing
less, breath's vapor barely

veiled that ceramic fleece;
it faced everything there was to see

inside and out
the sky-framing windowpane; one of a host

of dimestore knick-knacks seen daily while itself
seeing nothing, not the golden

neighborhood porches at noon nor the aluminum
sidings at evening going pale. Even so,

even as you know, have often imagined, the actual
scene sometimes near

irresistible: to stand at the high window
of the house across the street, overlooking it all

once more—the steps taken, the street played in—leaves you
inert, entombed, still

there is a light off a thing you look at sometimes
will let you see it open

with half an eye
from childhood you know you have not

seen the last of yet. . . .
Though our cells are renewed every seven years, you're no
    one

if not the one who was there
all along. When all else fails,

the sky sometimes permits this.

THIS IS THE BODILESS NIGHT

This is the bodiless night
when those who've loved no longer can

live as one wearing their flesh
with easy knowledge that it is common. . . .

Better leave
with a look which can see

better with eyes closed
than open,

and in walking, create
new space, each step

taken with no intention
of arriving, no expectation of place.

Or soon enough the level of memories stagnant
for so long begins

to shift,
and a mother's face, half-

dissolved, all the more
fills with craving

for its absent kiss, this
bodiless night, one

among many we don't know
until we see the not-yet-

outlived things we have not done
in order to live

the life we have, did, do, recalling all
too well what we won't be able to

at all later.

POVERTY

August. Anniversary. Marble stone.
Mother, underneath, alone,
as you watch the ball-turret fly on the window

swivel, lick its trigger-tooled forelegs
with rapid flicks of the tongue; delicate
armor-plated hinges, joints riveted with hair-

springs for instinctual flight. . . .What magic
is more precise! Looking on, you feel
you're about to enter somewhere within

a vast, impersonal patience laboring
without showing emotion or a heart
liable to breakage . . . plenty of feelers, though.

Sighting the snail's crawl, follow
a breath as it grows, so tranquil, close
to sleep; so sleepless,

a staring eye. Follow, if you can,
into bone marrow: how infinitesimal
cell-combs spend the honey our bodies hive

inside this liquid mine only
to have the ground
rush up to meet you or a prolonged

caving in, like an illness
that lays bare
untapped powers, richly

plowed, less than a moment
staying, the way happiness happens
quickly, all else slow.

THOSE AROUND US

They're all out there in the light
looking back that lays late
gold

leaf on the layered years. . . .
But the call comes from the dark:
"I would return to you,

if it were possible, the childhood you gave
with your manhood, had you not left
and taken it with you

into old age." And it's all
one to you where to begin
setting the tune

high or low above the sun-
lit harvest fallen
on hard times now that immensity's

reduced
to the beating of our hearts and oblivion
cruises

the backs of whoever
it pleases: those who see
in the calm now denied them

a hint
of what's to be granted later; how
it grows

more luminous
with each year
left behind; and those

for whom love is constant
dread that what has been and past is
better than what is going to be;

that all knowledge is paper
flesh pursuing power, and writing
kills in the end but keeps

you in the meantime
alive as night
draws near and the deep

agitations surface. And the faces no longer searched for
are carved now
from marble, from clay, from putty and mist

from here
on in. . . . Hold on. The line
forms to right and left for life-

jackets O falling
sailors who've never been on high
seas; for whom seeing and not

saying have become the same
as never having seen
one's real

face all along as you tow the foam-
threaded line, follow

the bouncing ball. . . .

A GIFT

For a long time now I have not been able to listen
to Dinu Lipatti's slender, ascetic fingertips
pressing ever so firmly gentle on the piano keys

in his last recorded transcription of Bach's Cantata
"Jesus bleibet meine Freude" given to me
by George Oppen the year he died.

                               It is too sad to hear
that severe, geometrically measured stroll of the soul
healthily light-stepping into heaven,

and has become sadder with each loved one's death:
the slow, spare, stately pace wrenching the heart
with its graceful ascendancy over grief,

and staring as if straight into the face of God
which is either everywhere or nowhere, leaving us
nothing to say, nothing to hear as luminous

and meltingly tender as the air
fills with silence, and the heart floods with loss.

FOR JOE CERAVOLO

As lightning turns
into itself whatever it strikes,
tonight in the long-distance dark

blot of your being let out of this
reality without end,
magical, mysterious, again

I read your poems, like sand flying
around an ocean, like nova
constellated between feelings,

their lean, virginal,
fast
forward jumps cut short goodbyes. Each

I, every you, can
fall. Down. Hard. Can
fall heavy. Down here, masonry leaning

toward fall, stirs through a slit
in the ski mask. In the sky, something
bright, like a wildflower in the dirt, dark

stain on the sun about to take
you in. Beautiful
bones that show through

the beak of being alive
reach out to reveal
the peaks

through the layers
that go as far
as you can

be open
who have drunk
reality to completion.

SHADES OF GRAY
—for Darrell

Out of the blue
bolts the not unexpected but still
shocking news, at forty-two, a last

photo of you, face so moonily
bloated with booze, pressing
your eyes closed. . . . And thus

you pass
from our outer
life to inner

where I see you again laughing it up
and down the alleys of the new
worlds, Iowa, California,

which you and the freebox-rummaging
street people used to pick through
for usable scraps . . . flower

power in rags . . .
as you told off the draft board:
"The only way you'll see me

in uniform
is as a soldier
in an invading army!"

•

Day unseasonably bright and long, pro-
longing the unknown in us, stretched
so thin to the horizon,

it shines. . . .
So shining
waits . . . light's

mute voice, bare
white flowing
page we enter,

we believe, for truth's sake,
and stay for the play
of syntax realigning sinews, quickening

synapse, singing airy
increase from
eye to hand, mouth to

mind, one
to another, stopping with no one,
but out of static and work—with luck—,

incantation spun
of our nerve-
ends' retuned symmetry, echoing, mirroring

melody's center within.
Haven't we known this hunger
from Adam? Haven't we got our work

cut out for us? To draw from
silence some remnant
sound we are,

willingly or not,
in the service of, all
one resonance moving

along with the source. . . .

        •

Bring that and more
here to air
out the time, the ache of

faceless space, staring
blind eye on all
we call on to oppose it. . . .

"To the first real space traveler,"
you wrote
of someone else.

Your name said it
all. Gray: shades of
black and white all colors

come from, go to finally
fade, dissolving clear
out to faint murmuring

star clusters farthest
ahead, cooled
source so long ago red-

shifted at the cusp as to be barely
there, where gravity's
a bottom-

less grave, placeless, restless, reck-
less flight never looking
away or back; no sound

barrier to break, no white
noise in blacklight, no time
to kill, no form but flight

from our thin hewn
radiance, free
of our

thin

held

line

AFTER SIX POEMS SET TO MUSIC
BY ANTON WEBERN

Song of a Trapped Blackbird
        —Georg Trakl

Golden step
                fading under the olive tree.
Aflutter with delirium wings the night.
How slowly humility must be bled;
        swelling dew rounded
        to a fall
                from the flowering thorn.

Growing, gathering arms hold up
                        a sinking heart.

•

The Sun
        —Georg Trakl

Every day the yellow sun comes over the hill.
Beautiful, the forest and the black beast, man;
    beautiful, the hunter and the herd.

Flashing red, a fish rises in the green pond.
Under vaulted heaven, in a blue boat
        a fisherman glides by.

Grapes leisurely ripen, and the grain.
When day winds down, and night falls,
The wanderer slowly lifts his heavy eyelids—
    sunlight darting from a dark ravine.

•

Occident I
    —Georg Trakl

Moon, as though a ghost
stepped from a blue grotto,
    blossom fallen
    across the rocky path.
All silvery, a sick thing weeps
    by the evening pool.

Ferried in droves, in a black boat deathward
    lovers go,
while Elis's footfalls sound now
    in the grove,
    now the hyacinth,
and die away under the oaks.

O for the hardness of the one
who turns a tear into crystal,
    shadow into night.

Lightning zigzags
    along temple walls,
and on the fattening hills
    spring storms run.

                    •

    At Night
                —Georg Trakl

The blue of my eye
    is less tonight
    than the red of my heart.
Yet how steadily the light holds!

Your blue covers the coming one;
Your red reveals the one gone,
    and those going on.

                    •

    Song
                —Rainer Maria Rilke

You alone make me.
You alone I can change with.
For a while it's you,

then again it's a rustle,
    a fragrance,
        disappearing.

Already all things here in my arms I hold
    and lose.
You only are always being born anew;
    because I never held you,
        you cannot be lost.

•

(After Hildegarde Jones)

Plunging from above comes the freshness that enlivens:
heart's blood is the moistness granted;
tears, the coolness given. How quickly they flow,
how quickly returned to the source
they flew from.
How privileged I am to also be where the sun is!
It loves me without reason,
I love it without end.
At evening we bid each other *auf Wiedersehen.*
Tomorrow, you who breathe will again be sunshine;
and you who sleep forever,
you too will see the dawn.

PART FOUR

CROSS-STREET

So much for the solid-
gold musical taste of the age,
                              upbeat, down
and out, love-
sick groans bawling
from the suitcase-sized boombox riding the shoulder
of a *cholo* in shades, webbed hairnet, flannel shirt
buttoned to the neck in midsummer; pimp-
strut rocking by on tip-
toe past pairs of squat, unisex
cops, hands on holsters, breezing as though the street's an
        open
bedroom, not book, closer
to sniffing whiffs of Opium, Taboo, off the dark necks' more
        darkly
bitten moons of unappeasable chicas; their wide, wing-
tipped eyes, salsa smiles night-shaded all
the way to the Bay of Angels. . . .

On Mission Street's sizzling McMeat rack,
past a punk blond with spiked hair tufts
speaking Queen's English; yakking
through a bullhorn's snout in an apostolic fit for the sheer
thumping hell of it, zeal-crazed, hormone-hit, a teenage kid
brandishing a black Bible beats the air
over pedestrians' heads. Soon as gawking
girls stop to stare, his hoarse voice cracks; no less
than everyone dropping in their tracks, on their knees
at his feet, penitential sobs, mass conversion will do
in full view of the born-again street. . . .

Through traffic and yak
without letup, listen: you can hear
those who promised to do away with history's
Alps on our backs now fighting for a place
in it; the old not letting go, the new
in tow, breaking
down, everywhere settling
for the nearest hole
to sink in,
                like anything pursued.

SIREN

A grown man's rough whimper—
muffled, baffled, and homely
as the face that moaned it in pure
misery must have been—as only

misery can plead, "But you said you liked me!" right
outside our bedroom window, loud
enough to wake us late one night
in that house in the old embattled neighborhood . . .

A lowdown, plaintive moan from deepest
registers and splashed, sawdust
floors; gutter-droppings scraped
raw from an aggrieved throat's lining; escaped

resonance from timbres of a despair
soaked in nightsweats and defeated
exhalations driven from the door.
Then the woman's voice, flat: "I needed

money"—firm, no frills, fucking
matter-of-fact, bringing on a chill
from a sleep no cavernous or sun-filled
dream could hold. I sensed the omen rocking

in a dead calm long before we moved.
In the black polluted pool of night, to be
pleading, shameless, miserably unloved,
wringing your heart out so that you see

and sense things you are not ever ready for
rush out of a vast, venomous indifference
having the whole engorged rat's ass
of night to yawn into! O most sorely missed: never-

to-be magic
moment of happiness of which we have not been a part.
Either way, there's the ultimate court
of speechlessness which can strike

even the most far-out, speed-rapping prince of sarcasm
dumb. Soon after we left, the oil-soaked, glass-strewn,
fume-filled, car-graveyard of a street—
gangs in doorways, shooters cruising by—would greet

neighbors and tourists alike, opening
a wider, hotter fire zone,
and every passing penetrating
sound, a variation of a siren.

POST-MODERNESQUE

"At the height of your powers,"
down on your luck,

sick, broke,
fugitive from flying

debris, from smoke, then fire, from one
burnt-out bomb-shelter reeking

hole in the wall to another web-
waving wall you face. . . .

Between the fire that forces flight
and the ice in which everything is fixed,

running to keep ahead
of the fire, and lingering to stare

into the ice, you
face the wall not the world

of tickets you stand in line for, groceries you buy,
which holds faith in a future that you don't. . . .

In homing intervals in a life
feeling like a breath sometimes

without a body, in rooms that take on
forms of your inwardness, rooms

reeking Lysol and exile, see
the dust itself collecting

crumbs, and a cement
tide rising in the throat, taste

of that rising
tide in which everything that aches

begs your useless allegiance. . . .
                              So, throw

yourself like dishwater into the street? grub
for the one thing on which so much depends? and (like all

those who are in this with you) we
so little command: surviving

the slum of kingdom come.
                              Luminous

ruin, ancient legacy famed
in our fantasy, leader of the band, lord without

visible body or baton, show us
the working heart in the breast of each one

that will cease, and the worlds along with them—
garden in the gardener's heart, ocean in the sailor's, sun

unbound from a woman's hair flowing
up ahead, without touching, drawing us who know

nothing until she looks our way. . . .
With a breath, spring

brushes her—visibly
last of our approaches to the god's

hindquarters in faded denim skirt—
urging us on to

urge her on to urge us:
stick around, see

the age of miracles come
to be a must again.

BLUE ZONES

Where instinct crosses
sparks at the cricket's synapse, there
spark I; streetwise, eye
level with the tumbling

soot's one-way ride
below the freeze-framed, nearly
touchable moon's bikini panty
taking forever to hit the floorboard
before the lights go dim

in the new car that drives like a humming
dove, and you humming
like a dove driving a dove
past the gleaming white marble
toilet of piety of a capital

where pious, beribboned
pissers all in a row review blueprints
they've dreamt of piloting, dropping
their payload through diamond

blue zones; on their faces the practiced
sorrow of men adrift at sea who grieve
for the fish they'll eat
even as they spear them. . . .

One look around tells you
all futures are bankrupt,
and those who promise them, the future's
bankers. All

in the flick of an oil man's eye
raised in calculation, piling on more
riches for the rich, rot for the rotten,
little for the little

lady, man, and nothing
at all for those who have nothing
but debts, taboos, the prolonged
Mongolian sadness, horseflies seven times
the color of dirt; for those who return
to the door they had closed behind, and knock,
and no one's in.

RADIO TEHRAN

Behold, whirling houris, in your shining hours
the nearing inferno and the numberless
miles more to be whirled up ahead! By your leaps

create the road, and the place where all that is
forbidden you here will be allowed you there
by the generous ancient hidden one

famous in your fantasy—new fruits, new perfumes, lovely
boys and lovely girls—as you weave
your way through gutters of the multitudes awash

in the world's glittering garbage! How much
they want, and how little
they want it to cost them! Your eager

fingertips tingling for the touch of taut
skin and drum, utterly now on your feet,
for the earth's tireless whirling will bring

you not a hairsbreadth closer. To pace it off
will wear out your shoes, to look for traces,
wear out your eyes. Rise,

shining houris, or from where you sit, circle
the oceans faster around than eyes fly open. Or
else, sink so deep memory cannot follow.

Much not granted here shall be granted there
that day when those amazed here
at what they see shall not be as amazed as you shall be.

THE HOME-FRONT

After the pin-
point fraction of concentrated hell-
fire is reined in and the generals

call off their air war on Baghdad, concrete-and-steel
rosette of a Babylonian garden
in the desert of my father's birth nearly wiped

from the earth, we watch
ragged, runny-nosed street Arabs
underneath aureoles of filthy curls

playing with live ammo in a minefield's mud,
their faces a play
of glance, grin, grimacing

moves too intent on their games to choose
caution over curiosity. . . .
Sunlight is their only vitamin.

Turning to the camera, their wide
eyes withdraw, filling with darkness
against the light off the dunes.

If eyes don't lie,
who will not see his own
child's face in theirs, stark

beauty of things in peril, more alarmingly
alive looking out of the ditch
than we looking in?—the Law

like a loaded gun trained upon them.
Who, if he could, would give up his seat
and go down and look

through those eyes at the darkness so suddenly
fallen, Abraham's knife still
slicing the air down

the blue sky their bodies would be made of
if only the absentee Lord
God, against all evidence, were to return, bewitch

sweet water from the salty sea
and create us right for once?
Promises and prayers come

to nothing. Each day we act against our blood-
bond with the other side and manage to hide
the shame of having abandoned it. . . .

Such is the scent of the sulfurous
present on the home-front:
everything racing at increasing speed

toward the opposite of what we intended.

BLOOD IN THE FACE

Blackened from having passed through billowing
fuel-dragons devouring air, come
news-photo dots made of desert sand, together

drawing the familiar picture:
cowering victims, curried victor;
but these victims embrace and kiss

their executioner, à la Française; flushed
blood drawn into his face, drained from
theirs who gaze enraptured on the grinning

lord of life and death. And we, struck by the glimpse
of a god in their gaze, are ourselves in the presence
caught up. Like watching your ancestors

eating royal shit and craving it. Remember,
like them, when you thought there was no point
in going on, then realized it was all

an endless, emptying string of indignities,
and you would not be exempt from any of it; not
the writhing of a slug on a steak, nor the gradual

slow sinking, luxuriant
as sesame in honey. Now watch
the blushing butcher demur, so

convincingly shy, doubtless deeply
touched to his fatty bones
for all to see, unveiled

virgin bride never embraced, never
kissed so ardently before.
Makes the skin crawl, seeing

how flesh instinctively knows
the feel of this oily, under-heel
worming for its life

from other incarnations, all eager
to be deluded and let the heart's rage dilute
its venom and be eaten to contrition. . . .

Submission, too, has its raptures,

or are they, in his embrace, already turning
away with one foot and reaching
forward with the other, greased

feet at the summit
before the downward slide?
Though you sacrifice yourself, nothing will remain

of the offering but smoke.
When the dust settles,
we'll be ashes.

IN THE SHADOW OF THE POISONED WIND

In Arctic latitudes, almost another
planet, Laplanders herd their radiation-
laden reindeer down from their mountain

feeding grounds. Without a sound now
they glide like robes of royalty, billowing, breathing
sleeves of vapor, tiara antlers, thick

fur glowing dark as mahogany
fattened on vegetation watered by nuclear rains.
To be slaughtered, and not eaten. So we

go into what has been gliding
forward to meet us from so long ago
we have seen coming against the black

velvet of galactic space,
the many pouring down to the one
wave not yet broken. Shadow

on ice, here and gone.

NOTE

at the window: ragged butterfly
wings snagged three days in a spiderweb still
flutter in the corner, torn
bit of brown crepe in a breeze. . . .

Nothing special, or
else a revelation if after a minute's long
look you see in miniature,
stubbornly, barely,
a kilowatt of energy
trying to pull free, still faintly
warm with instinct in the finespun maw. . . .

And later see on captured newsreel
the enemy pilot shot down
onto the crowded street, the enraged mob
beating him bloody, swollen
pulp face, flopping arms, a rag doll's
stuffing showing through,
and wonder if the brain has yet triggered
its morphine to null the pain. . . .

And the son's father alone in his apartment
in the Holy City, seeing it on TV
saying, "In the dream
of my life, this is the nightmare."

FROM THE BIG BRASS HANDBOOK: CHAPTER 2

Into yourself take
this down. Listen,
we are giving you centuries
worth of tips in a few moments'
briefing. . . .

     Pick up, if you can,
the tune on your guts'
acoustic ax and stone-
wall the duped mother-
fucking numb-nuts'
law-abiding brains
until they're baffled
blue in the face and take
a different tack: one less
opposed to our interests. . . .

     Hooked back
from inner space as soon as you wake
in the morning you know
you're not going to have your dream that day
and the day just begun
in millennium fever
rushing outside into the next
not yet begun. . . .

     Now hear this:
we are the spirit of the most
new thing there is and want

to share the newness with you,
and though the God of your
fathers, that fading elusive
print like Bigfoot's, is nowhere
in sight, there's a parrot here
robed in the cloak of law and order
who knows a few words
of his language. By the book,
by the balls, he gives you as much
justice as you can afford. . . .

       Old veteran, on your own
like a child
frozen in the center
of a man on the run, have you felt
today a love for the ordinary
to the point of revolution? Have you
felt a power, unsettling
with all the imperative of the moment,
pounce? . . .

       It's not hard; living
through a day's not hard, if you can live
through a moment. Imagination creates
despair with its millions
of future moments, thousands of awaited days, so
draining, blurring, you can't see
the moment or hand before you. . . .

       Remember,
all work not your work is serving
time in someone else's slammer.

In your cell, staring
into pits your own or other hands have
opened, you'll notice
how soon captives begin speaking
like their captors; how,
for the terrorized, the pardoned
from pity, just beginning to feel
the least bit easeful, the light strikes deeper
terror than the dark. . . .

How on the outside, as warring
gangleaders and governments signing
peace treaties are headlined as heroes,
assassination has become the sin-
cerest form of flattery, while the privileged few grab
for what's phony and the rest line up
for imitation phony. Pig-
lets squealing for Parnassus.

Is it any wonder
nerves and palates demand stronger
doses of the monumental, while those
who have nothing to say
because the Uzi squeezes
out the last word, keep hurling
their theories at each other, mangling
the few mixed feelings they'll be mass
buried with along with the leaden-
tongued Don Juans, the lotus-
lipped yonis fixed to their sides, leaning
over backward to pour
blessings on their downfall; from bliss

to breakdown in a moment's
slide not one step away
from where you are now, in the ruins
elevated to shrines in the eyes
of the enervated
veterans of romance. . . .

While everything we do focuses
on winning, they're satisfied
too soon, or, to the tune of

"May the truth touch you
not with its terrible teeth,"
they moan the loss of a past
richer, sweeter,
while blinded to the quickly shrinking
bid of the evaporating
present, boogying to it
as the beer suds they guzzle long
gone flat before it was barreled. . . .

Listen,
avoid the spotlight; you'll do
better work when no one pays
any attention. And if what you come up with
is not what you've experienced, perhaps
it's prophecy speaking through you all
tongues at once. . . .

Stay in shape, be wily:
if ill, make illness your ally.
Illness can be a kind of space

travel one longs to return from. When you do,
it's to a new planet, in a new season,
in a new form. It's better
than leaving your body
to science
while still in it. Better
than the survivor of the Warsaw ghetto
saying, "If you could lick my heart
it would poison you."

       Whoever takes this
hook need not look any further. Look
only for this fishhook; the more
caught you are, the more free. . . .

       It only remains
to wish you good luck
in this age in which it's possible will be shown
did not exist. . . .

UNDER A CLOUD AS BIG AS A STATE

Season of the urge at year's end to bring
something to conclusion, when each day's earlier
darkening feels long as a season,

now the lean stripping wind
drawn by the striped green dragon
comes in battering

black
tattered
beading down

rain-slick bark, darkening
leaves, broadening shadows, muting all
under the eaves but the bright

red
cyclamen's tongue-
tip

alone
in the garden's corner calling up
going and the soon

to be gone, fragile
bright eye-
catching petals, delayers of death, sharpening

goodbye, while as near as
a moment ago you could feel all shapes
around the freesias' lemon-scented

silkiness in the vase draw close
because the gaze traveling over them
could be one's last. . . .

                              To our retinas all things return
the color they reject . . . high heaven
refuses blue . . . so the visible brings and space takes

the world away.
                              And it's going
to be hard

asking at the eleventh hour
that our words echo
more than their brief longing;

there'll have to be a going far
when she leaves the room and the full
weight of you goes down

one more story in sadness.
Then the heart's small
handful of immensity

will have to beat beyond
the inherited crowded corridors we're filled with, and gone
as far as possible, all

you turned away from, your worst
fear takes on a face
suspiciously familiar,

flashed
before your inner
eye in moments briefly

awake, as if fate were
glimpsed in blinking
flashes, a smear, slow-mo . . .

And the generations that went
into their making now you see
all the way fast

forward to. . . . As in sickness,
weaving our wavelengths
back into ourselves,

we're brought supinely
solo for a while
to where we've come from

and (the years wearing
away, rich, menacing
and swift, becoming more

rich with menace)
go.
          How

take cover
from what comes at you
from all sides, or hide

from what never goes away?—
with no logic
that does not weary of its rock, no

traffic that does not go
but wild, no change of heart
except in an air running

backward
in the dragon's tail. . . .
                              Faster,

everything's become
faster so there'd be more time, and
there's less

time now than ever. . . .
You're growing quieter
without noticing, harder

without meaning to, jotting
fewer entries in
The Notebook of Exquisite Things

in the effort to stare
danger down until the details take on
intensity, magic

rather than the everyday
remedy that works, the everyday
luxury paid for with poverty.

It must be a twinge
on my accelerating
way to forgetfulness that sets me to thinking—

we who are living the last years
of a century possessed
by all the goodwill of a wolf

may still glimpse
beyond the streets laid out for targeting
and the alien, haunted

head of the moving column,
how nothing short of throwing
ourselves out of our eyes'

open window will let us see all which keeps
us from falling is that we were
never on solid ground to begin with.

COLOPHON

The text of this book was set in Dante type. Coffee House books are printed on acid free paper and are smyth sewn for durability and reading comfort.